Chopsticks For My Noodle Soup

CHOPSTICKS FOR MY NOODLE SOUP

ELIZA'S LIFE IN MALAYSIA

BY SUSAN E. GOODMAN

Photographs by Michael J. Doolittle

The Millbrook Press   Brookfield, Connecticut

To Lee, Molly, Julia, and Nikki—
the best bunch of nieces and nephews

S.G.

To Eliza: Every day, no matter where
we are, I feel lucky to be her Dad.

M.D.

Library of Congress Cataloging-in-Publication Data
Goodman, Susan E., 1952—
Chopsticks for my noodle soup : Eliza's life in Malaysia / by Susan Goodman;
photographs by Michael Doolittle.
p. cm.
Summary: A photographic record of a five-year-old Connecticut girl's
year in a remote village in eastern Malaysia.
ISBN 0-7613-1552-7 (lib. bdg.)
1. Malaysia, East—Social life and customs—Pictorial works—Juvenile literature.
[1. Malaysia—Social life and customs.] I. Doolittle, Michael J., ill. II. Title.
DS597.333.G66   2000
959.5'3—dc21   99-30565   CIP

Published by The Millbrook Press, Inc.
2 Old New Milford Road
Brookfield, Connecticut 06804
www.millbrookpress.com

y name is Eliza. I live with Mama and Daddy in New Haven, Connecticut—most of the time.

This year, Mama had to work in a country called Malaysia. So Daddy and I went, too. It took us two whole days and five different airplanes to get there.

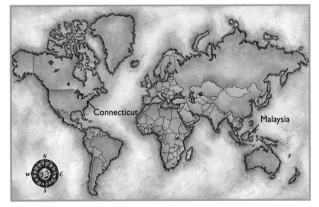

There is no snow in Malaysia. It feels like summer most of the time.

When we take walks here, we count water buffalo instead of squirrels.

In Malaysia, they have water taxis. And jungles.

A lot of things are different.

In Malaysia, we have a fence around our house so the cows can't come in. I like using the ladder to climb over it instead of opening the gate.

Cows can't come in, but chickens visit me from all over the village. I feed them leftover rice. Once I found an egg on our steps, and we scrambled it for lunch. Now I search for them first thing every morning.

Our house is on stilts. Dad says they're important because they keep it above the mud and water during the rainy season. I like them because they mean I can have a swing right underneath my house!

Every morning when I get up, I have to go outside to get to the bathroom. When I first saw it, I thought, Wow, who lives in such a little house?

I didn't even know what to do in there until Mama showed me. You have to squat down over this flat toilet. Then, since it doesn't have a flusher, you pour in some water and it all kind of slips away.

A lot of people here eat rice for breakfast. I like French toast. I put honey on it, though. They don't have maple syrup in Malaysia.

I drink orange juice for breakfast, but we make it out of powder and water that we've boiled on the stove. You see, nobody in our village drinks water right from the faucet. We cook it first to get the ants and germs out.

We also use boiled water for brushing our teeth. Then we spit that water out the doorway. I never got to do that before.

When it's time to go to kindergarten, a neighbor often gives us a ride to school. He lifts us onto his truck where we can all move around. No seatbelts!

Before we go into the school, we take off our shoes. People almost never wear shoes inside a house in Malaysia. It's just the way they do things here.

I'm glad. I like walking around in my bare feet. And it's not really my fault when my socks get dirty.

In school we sit at desks most of the time. We practice writing our letters and words like *kuching* (cat), *keribau* (water buffalo), and *pisang* (banana). *Monyet* is the Malaysian word for monkey. It reminds me of the way we say it in English.

At first, it was hard to be with some of the kids at school. They would come up to me and grab my arm or put their hands on my head. Mama said that's because they think I am special. I look different from them, so they want to touch my skin and feel my light hair.

I didn't like it. Their fingers got tangled in my hair and it hurt. I wanted to say something, but I didn't know how. So Mama and I practiced saying, "*Jangan!*" That means, "Don't!" in their language.

I've made new friends, but that was hard at first. I wanted to say, "Hello, let's play," and I didn't know how. I tried talking to some girls, but they kept speaking their own language. So I smiled instead.

Finally, when I saw all the other kids having fun, I just started to play, too.

We don't pack a lunch for school; it's not the custom. They make us lunch instead. I hate the soup; it's too full of boiled onions. But the brown rice with sauce is so good. Sometimes they even mix noodles and rice together.

Best of all, the cook sells us candy any time we want it.

Older kids go to school all day long, but we leave after lunch. At the end of every day, we line up to shake hands with *Cikgu Anna*. That means "Miss Teacher Anna" in English.

Sometimes we leave school and run all the way home. But sometimes we stop to jump over cow pies. I call it the "cow flop hop."

In Malaysia, they say, "Have a safe journey," when they want to say good-bye. I taught my new friends another way. We blow each other kisses.

Some afternoons I help wash our clothes in the river. It's not so hard. You put soap on the clothes and scrub them with a brush. Then you hold them in the river to rinse out the soap.

Once I lost a sock and it started to float away. When I went after it, I fell all the way in.

"Hold on," said Daddy, and he brought me and the sock back to shore.

We take our clean clothes back home and hang them on a rope to dry. If we don't watch the sky, sometimes the clothes just get wetter. It rains a lot in Malaysia.

Mama studies how the people here use their forests. Her work takes her into the jungle, and sometimes I go along.

The first time you go into the jungle, you just see green, green, green. But once you get what Daddy calls "jungle eyes," you can find some really amazing things.

SUMATRAN PIT VIPER

LEAF-FOOTED BUG

ORCHID

21

There aren't any supermarkets in our town; they have *tamus* instead. A *tamu* is like an outdoor store that comes to the village once a week. That's the day we go shopping.

You can buy soap and clothes and all kinds of things to eat—even chickens that are alive. You are supposed to kill them at home and eat them. We have never gotten one. We don't want to.

But we do take home new foods to try. I like the tiny bananas and fruits called pomelos and the rice cakes that are sweet and chewy.

The *tamu* is lots of fun. Sometimes we see men playing gongs that sound like drums with echoes. They are so loud, you hear them with your whole body.

But the sound I like best is when I hear the words, "*Ais Krim.*" That's what the ice-cream man says when he rides up on his motorcycle.

Lots of times I help make dinner. Our kitchen is a separate building next to our house, just like the bathroom. Sometimes we have *nasi goreng* (fried rice) for dinner, or even fried squash blossoms. I really miss hamburgers.

When we have noodle soup, I practice using chopsticks. But then I cheat and finish with a spoon.

Our house in Malaysia has chairs and a couch. In other homes, people sit on the floor, even at dinnertime. They eat on the floor, even if they have a table.

I like our house, but I like theirs, too. When there is hardly any furniture, my friends and I can run around really fast without stopping.

In Malaysia, they celebrate lots of holidays like the Harvest Festival and Chinese New Year.

This year, we're celebrating what Mama calls "our Malaysian Christmas." There is no snow, and we couldn't find a Christmas tree to cut down. So we had to buy a fake one. But we still found plenty of things we could decorate it with.

And, luckily, Santa Claus goes to every country there is.

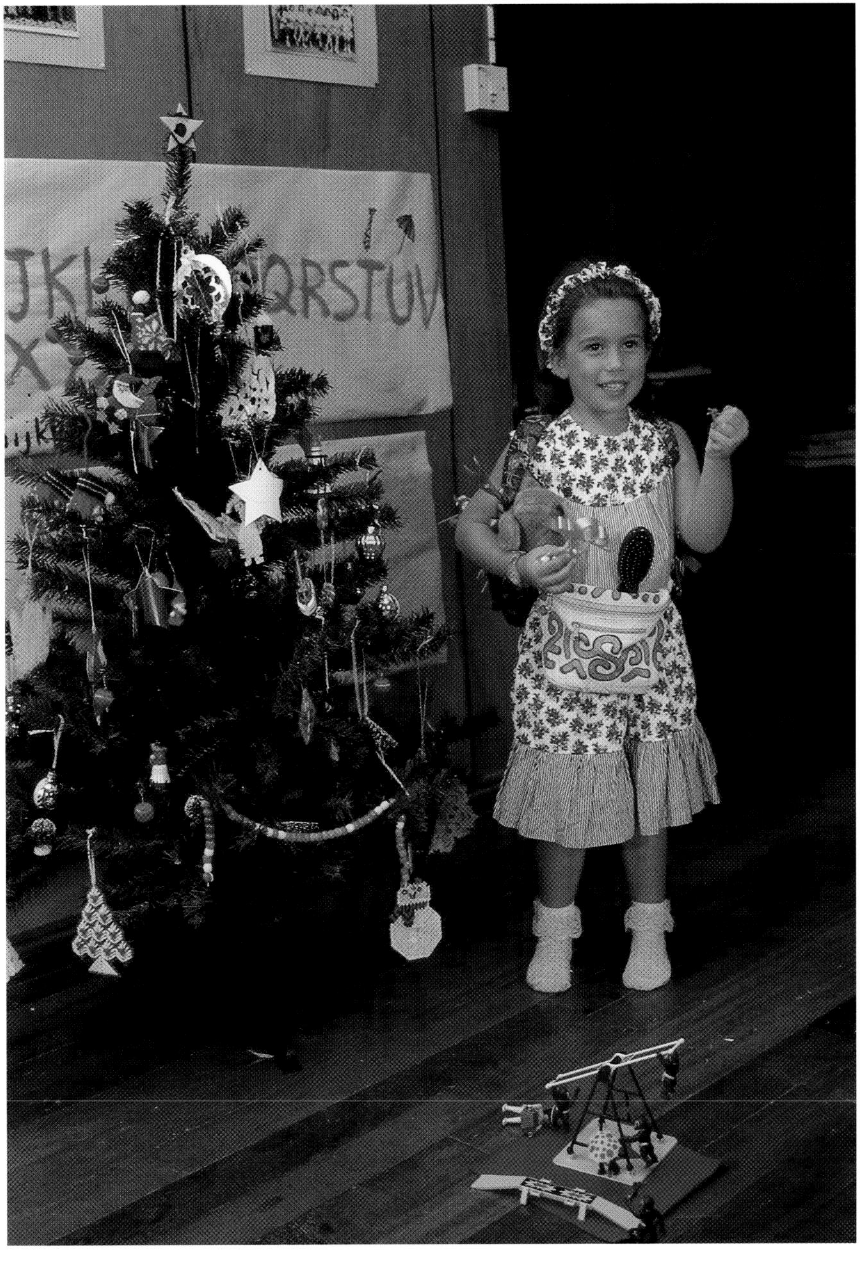
JKL
QRSTUV

On Christmas Eve, just like every other night, we heat up water so I can take my bath.

Then I go to bed under my mosquito netting. Lisa, my teddy bear, comes with me. She goes everywhere I go, even to Malaysia. Sometimes Lisa gets a little homesick for America. But then I cuddle up and tell her that as long as she's with us—with me and Mama and Daddy—she's at home.

31

McLEAN COUNTY UNIT #5
105-CARLOCK

About the Author and Photographer

Susan Goodman and Michael Doolittle have collaborated on many books, including the Ultimate Field Trip Series (*Ultimate Field Trip 1: Adventures in the Amazon Rain Forest*; *Ultimate Field Trip 2: Stones, Bones, and Petroglyphs: Digging into Southwest Archaeology*; *Ultimate Field Trip 3: Wading into Marine Biology*; and *Ultimate Field Trip 4: Stepping into the Past*).

Susan Goodman is also the author of *Unseen Rainbows, Silent Songs: The World Beyond Human Senses* and *Wildlife Rescue*. She writes magazine articles for adults and kids as well. Susan wishes she could have seen Malaysia with the Doolittles, although she would have missed her own family in Boston, Massachusetts.

Photographing his daughter was a labor of love for Michael Doolittle, but his professional expertise was well matched to the project. He has photographed children in action for such magazines as *National Geographic World* and *Outside Kids* as well as for the books he has done with Susan. The Doolittles are back from Malaysia and eating their noodle soup with spoons in New Haven, Connecticut.